CRACKING UP

by Jennifer L. Manlowe, PhD

For my nieces

Taylor Bryant, Megan Manlowe, Maria Manlowe,

Lauryn Bryant, Alyssa Manlowe

"We of the craft are all crazy."—*Lord Byron*

CONTENTS
ACKNOWLEDGMENTS

PART V
Truly cracked up!
Clearing out the clutter
Has my heart gone to sleep?
I do not write in order to be right!

ACKNOWLEDGMENTS

To all my friends and family-members that
continue to encourage me to keep writing, thank
you! CJ Dorgeloh, Whitney Bennett, Danielle
Doughman, Melinda Manlowe, Pearl Helms, Nancy
Lewis, Mary Cappello, Jean Walton, Rhonda
Goolsby, Tanya Gisa, Laury Bryant, Susan
Kuebler, Carol Corbus, Diane Kobrynowicz,
Valerie Young, Barbara Winter, Jan Schwer and
Janine Fixmer. My fiercely grateful heart also goes
to my fondest encourager and sweetest song,
Tony Fairbank. Last and not least, my nieces: the
wickedly-brilliant girrrls, Megan, Maria and Alyssa
Manlowe and their sassily-wise cousins, Taylor
and Lauryn Bryant. The indomitable Molly
Manlowe will be able to read this when she reaches
her teens (about 12 years from now!).

PART I

I SWEAR, THIS IS ALL TRUE

"If the truth is stranger than fiction, print the fiction."—*Anonymous*

Dear nieces and interested-readers:

Be warned: *Cracking Up* is a girrrlbook[1] written in the form of a letter by that growling girrrl in me who cannot tell a lie. Oh yes, that "girrrrl" is really a fully grown woman—born January 28th 1963—whom my nieces call "Auntie Jenn" or "Tía Margarita"— depending on the season. That girrrl-woman, my nieces' Auntie, will now recollect almost all the peculiar advice she has received regarding: "What makes a young girl a successful woman?" Most, if not all of this unsolicited advice, has

---

[1] Girrrl = the kind of girl that isn't afraid to growl like a tiger when she feels so inclined, i.e., when she's threatened, hungry, desirous or protective.

come from her relatives, family-friends and even from some well-meaning, oddly-empowered strangers.

The medium for this recollection is that oh-so-antiquated vehicle called "the Letter." Sometimes, within this letter, I will include a furtive missive, a pithy quote, or a direct note of warning. Other times this text will read like a short-history "sidebar" or a brief scene from a play. Still, at other times, the reader will be invited to use her[2] imagination: she'll feel moved to invent an alternative future as if beckoned by some kind of oracle figure who floats just above her head. She may even feel

---

[2] I have chosen to use the feminine pronoun (generically) because the reader is presumed to be female; I am writing to my nieces, after all. Plus, I thought it would be "simpler" for the read to skip the bulkiness of "he/she" – This is an excuse made by millions of authors that have chosen to have "he/his/him/man/mankind" be an adequate umbrella for humankind.

as if her own life-force depended on disentangling herself from a dastardly spell! But, remember, each story told in this lengthy letter is absolutely true. Some of the names and details have been changed to appease my very sensitive and guilt-ridden Momma, but the facts remain the same. Each bit of counsel was actually given to me, each tale was earnestly told to me, and I'm sure, all this advice was conveyed under the benign auspices of wanting to steer little ole' me toward *true fulfillment as a female*. So, please readers, and especially my nieces, pay close attention or bear the consequences!

Many women of the 21st century (and even a few men) might find that they will recollect being taught these fables and fibs of feminine fantasia. My nieces: Meagan, Taylor, Lauryn, Alyssa and Maria (five girls aged 14-17) may giggle with glee at the outrageous messages given to me—someone they call "brave, independent, sassy, a little crazy and even *an outlaw*"—due to living outside the laws of *The Holy See.*[3]

Perhaps readers who are not my nieces will laugh with the girrrls as I recall the tidbits of "wisdom" bestowed to me from around age four on up to the present (45).

My primary hope is that we begin "cracking up" with laughter as we read these stories together rather than end

---

[3]**Holy See** is the papacy or the papal court; those associated with the pope in the government of the Roman Catholic Church at the Vatican; all so called See of Rome.

up "cracking up" mentally by trying to follow such antiquated, even grisly girl counsel.

Girrrls, guess what I have uncovered? After writing my first draft of this book, I searched all the online libraries to see if my title was in use by some other author. To my surprise, I discovered that *Cracking Up*—this book— sounds just a little bit like that *other* award-winning author's book. You may remember him, F. Scott Fitzgerald, the author of *The Great Gatsby*? Anyway, he also wrote a book with a similar title to my own and he was 42 at the time (close to my same age). In his book, *The Crack Up*, he attempted to warn his only daughter about life and the illusions of glamour, glitz and the glory promised by his own cultural moment in this, his final work. So, in a way, we shared a similar passion and mission in our writing.

In a series of three essays published by *Esquire Magazine* in 1936, Fitzgerald made attempts to bear his soul to the world at large for letting them—and himself—down. His book begins:

"Of course all life is a process of breaking down, but the blows that do the dramatic side of the work—the big sudden blows that come, or seem to come, from outside—the ones you remember and blame things on and, in moments of weakness, tell your friends about, don't show their effect all at once. There is another sort of blow that comes from within— that you don't feel until it's too late to do anything about, until you realize with finality that in some regard you will never be as good a man again."

Girrrls, it is important that you know that my book, *Cracking Up*, is in no way a confessional speech or a maudlin "looking back" upon roads not taken. Nor is it a "morality tale" by a besotted and dejected artist in search of renown. Rather, I hope this work will be one among many future works that function more as an inoculation than resignation to such hopelessness. Perhaps it might even interrupt any future disappointment born of chasing the ersatz American-Dream or disrupt the fallacious promises of a "happily-ever-after" melodrama of marriage."[4]

As you must know, girrrls, divorce is just as likely to make you happy as marriage. To wit: divorce statistics tell us we have a "50-50"

---

[4] For more on that kind of critique of consumer-spirituality, see my book *Loving Life as it Is* (Life Design Inc., 2006).

chance at this particular route to happiness. What intelligent person puts her future in the hands of a surgeon who is successful only 50% of the time?

A FOUR-PART OUTLINE

First of all, girrrls, I have a four-part agenda to this letter: (1) to illustrate just how universal the myth of romantic fulfillment is, then (2) to help you uncover the other myths that haunt the lives of females (straight or lesbian), (3) to encourage you to keep your eyes' out for the fault-line running throughout popular fantasies, consumer culture and the bulk of modern media. After that, I intend (4) to give you evidence of this *folie à deux*—madness shared by two—from my own life. But, in the end, girrrlies, I trust you draw your own conclusions and find your own resonances with the outrageous experiences in this book. As they say in Alcoholics Anonymous, "Take what you like and leave the rest!" Perhaps you'll write a letter to me offering your own version of what it's been like for you to grow up as a plucky[5] girl who survived the mixed messages of her times.

Let's begin to take a long hard look at the "cult of true love." Does this cult set people up to fail? Do you know one person who has found true contentment with love for just one person? I find that I can't swing a squirrel without hitting a person who has betrayed or, more commonly, disillusioned by the promise

---

[5] Showing determined courage in the face of difficulties.

of one true love! Let's pull back the curtain in the Land of Oz, shall we?

BUT WITHOUT A MAN...

"You're only half a woman!" said Momma as she snubbed out her cigarette on my half-eaten plate of scrambled eggs.

"I swear, I didn't make that up!" she shouts, "look it up in one of those philosophy books!"

Growing up in the 1960s, I experienced my Momma as complex, even Janus-like (with two different faces). On the one hand, she seemed eager to have my sister, my female cousins and myself learn whatever there was to learn about the world as if life were one great big adventure. On the other side of the coin, she seemed to want us to learn even more quickly that our value as girls came in direct proportion to our surface impression— how attractive we appeared to the outside world. This was the same kind of vexed advice she received from her own mother (you girls know her as "Big Sissy"), the guardian of both conservative and bohemian values, who also seemed to have two distinct sides of herself from which she drew forth such "wisdom."

JANUS
God of Beginnings

Two heads back-to-back represent Janus looking in opposite directions. Ironically, Janus **only appeared** to be "two-faced" on the coin commemorating him. He was the Roman god known as 'the custodian' (Janitor) of the universe. He is the god of beginnings and the guardian of gates and doors. In his right hand he holds a key. He was worshipped at the beginning of planting time, harvest, marriages, births and other important beginnings in a person's life. Maybe his "vibes" will bless the important beginning of this book.

Kittens, if Momma were here right now she would add, "Oh, Jay Z., you know that I never gave you girls such mixed-up messages! Big Sissy and I have always said that 'good looks will only get you so far!'" Momma did tell me that, "Every woman needs to have some sort of professional skill—like typing—to *fall back on* just in case her husband dies or becomes debilitated in some way!" This "profession-to-fall-back-on" for Momma was, at first, English literature, something she adored. She couldn't get enough Shakespeare, Chaucer, Pope and Marlowe.

In the first semester of her senior year of college, Momma panicked and decided to switch her attention from getting straight A's in English to getting a more marketable degree in "personnel" [now called "Human Resources"]. That final year, Momma crammed all the available HR data into her brain and excelled at all the required courses in personnel training, shorthand and typing classes to become the speediest secretary, or Personal Assistant, 1956 could spit out of the University of Washington.

Again, the messages were mixed for all. For instance, reading was always encouraged by example in Momma and Big Sissy's family. While I was growing up, Momma would often have a book *in each hand* as a passenger during longer car trips. Words and knowledge of their meaning mattered a great deal. Both she and Big Sissy had the habit of urging me to look up unfamiliar words—and their etiology—in Webster's largest dictionary or Britannica's children's encyclopedia – a rainbow collection that broke up the beige atmosphere of our faux-wood, paneled family room.

Poor Momma, this passion for reading complicated her Betty Crocker aspirations. [FYI: "Betty" was 1921's fictional version of "Martha Stewart" without the insider-trading debacle.] But, to Momma's chagrin, cheerfully playing the role of "most-satisfied-wife and mother" was a social mandate, a *non-negotiable*, for all white middle-class women in the post-war 1950s. Most women of color at this time, on the other hand, never stopped working both in and outside the home—some

as teachers and secretaries and the majority
as low-wage, service workers.

As a white, middle-class, Catholic woman,
Momma was not unique in having to sacrifice
her intellectual appetite for the socially-
acceptable demands of husband and family.
Even though Momma's parents were agnostic,
somewhere she read that there was "a divine
order" or "naturalness" in marriage. I believe
she said something like this: "Men and women
will always seek *their other half* because they
used to be *One*." Momma said there was a
mythological character that reflected the first
human being who was at once male and female.

Was Momma referring to "Adam" in Genesis?
Hebrew scholars sometimes refer to this first

human figure as "Adaam" (meaning "creature," in Hebrew)? Adaam was considered to be the original human being: "male and female God created them" (Genesis 2:6).[6]

The other idea could have come from Momma's stumbling across one of Big Sissy's comparative religion books where she saw illustrated an Indian or Hindu god/des named

"Uma-Maheswra." Uma-Maheswra was considered to be a human *gynandromorphy* whereby half the deity's body appeared to have

[6] See Phyllis Trible's God and the Rhetoric of Sexuality.

female characteristics and the other half,
male.

Momma's sense of destined "original
oneness" could have come from her basic
understanding of Darwin's single-cell theories
of origins. Then again, she may have been
referring to Aristotle's homunculus (below):
this is character that was supposedly *sui
generis*—unto itself—a little male creature
planted in the womb that only "turned" female
if, through the birthing process, it was
deformed. The female, for Aristotle was
called "a misbegotten male."

 Aristotle believed that an utterly preformed human, that he called "Homunculus," took the shape of a little seed. This itty-bitty seed was planted by its "Sire," the fertilizing male, into the inert field-bed or "soil" of a female's womb. This fully-formed creature was thought to merely increase in size to become a baby over the course of nine months of gestation. In the image (credit: Bryan Crockett) the homunculus is proportioned this way because humans have different sensitivity for various portions of the body (i.e., the hands, the lips or the sexed organ are much more sensitive than the abdomen).

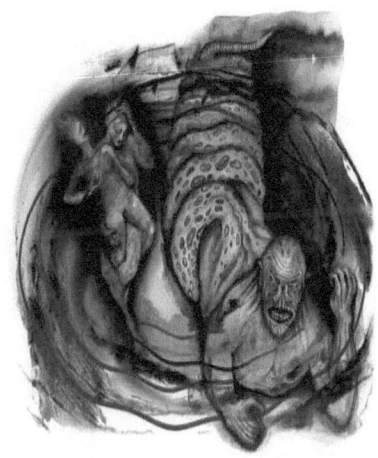

There is another famous myth about male-female "divine union" that is quite the opposite of Eden's "original bliss." Instead of damning the lust-filled creatures to a life-long fate of searching for their "missing half" for all eternity, Dante's deity actually grants the wishes of the two voracious lovers who long to "be together forever" (Circle 2, Canto 5). Their prayers are hellishly-answered; they will now share an enmeshed fate eternally as their made-to-order punishment in his *Inferno*. Cultural myths work on so many levels and this "longing-for-wholeness" through sacred union has had many repercussions for almost all the women in Greek (Western) history.

Because we are Western raised, we are influenced by Western myths and these tales have also influenced Biblical myths, like Genesis's creation story. Did you know that Momma and Big Sissy, though not reared as "Bible Believers" nor Churchgoers of any stripe, were still brought up to seek paradise outside themselves through romantic love— i.e., merging with a man? Did you think they even knew they were being misled, even brainwashed, through radio, TV soap operas, and later, every 1950s matinee they sat through? Mercy, what *normal* (always assumed heterosexual) girl wouldn't want the screen lives of Grace Kelly, James Dean, Rita Hayworth, Elizabeth Taylor, Montgomery Cliff, Natalie Wood, Rock Hudson, Jane Wyman, Joanne Woodward and Paul Newman [1/3rd of these actors were, in fact, gay]?

These Hollywood characters became Momma's personal Greek pantheon to the netherworld. But this tragic fantasy life had its consequences. I will lay out of few of them for you here. But first, have compassion for Momma and Big Sissy because this was their world.... Do fish know they are swimming in water? Momma and her Momma were blind to the hypnotic powers of this anesthetizing world in which they swam. Think of Dorothy trying to stay clear-headed while traipsing through those Poppy Fields.

What girl could resist psychically-*purchasing* the versions of romantic love that she saw plastered all over the popular magazines and dime store novels?—not unlike *Harlequin Romance* novels in my day. Romantic love to most middle-class women in Momma's day was tantamount to buying a *lotto ticket* for the newly-unemployed steelworker. Both "tickets," if won, promised dreams of unlimited happiness and prosperity. The lure of such a game was unremitting— because, as my friend Tracy says, "The longest lasting love is the unrequited kind."

The truth is, such bliss is always out of reach, and this disillusionment is felt most pointedly when it is "won."

Like the fantasies of the American Dream, Momma thought her marriage to my father (Poppa Manlowe) would promise her total fulfillment—eternal happiness—through becoming a wife and mother of four (the size of her original family, a model that she wanted to replicate).

Just like other white, middle-classed, straight girls of her time period, Momma was raised on Post WWII material-idealism. Where bigger, faster, more was tantamount to "better."

Poor Momma, I remember watching her friends dabbing their damp eyes at weddings. They would look longingly at the bride's crinoline dress and gaze up (always up) at the starched shirt of the groom and his groomsmen. These women, in their own way, seemed to be running from their lived realities: faithless marriages to alcoholics, gamblers, debtors, embezzlers, absent fathers, verbally-aggressive, emotionally-cruel or even abusive men. As I think about it now, female tears at many weddings seem to be about a weighty disappointment that cannot be shaken off— as if such heaviness were the last ten, recalcitrant pounds of a diligent dieter.

It should come as no surprise to learn that Momma always spoke of needing to "drop ten pounds," the same ten pounds that Big Sissy needed to gain. In fact, both women were always on one *miracle diet* or another—at least publicly and, sometimes, in front of each other like some kind of not-so-secret *smackdown* competition. The heaviness Momma felt as a virtually-single, mother-of-four, (with one child extremely, developmentally disabled), was never spoken of as a problem. Rather, the only struggle that was ever vocally acknowledged, by herself and her mother, seemed to be a "stubborn weight problem" that each could never properly manage.

What woman wouldn't feel heavy-hearted, irritably-bloated and flooded with the flow of mixed messages running like "ticker-tape" through her head: "Find your other half!" "Be

able to manage on your own … *just in case.*"
"With hard work, and by purchasing all these
time-saving new appliances, you too can live
the American Dream!" "More is always better!"
"You can never too rich or too thin!" "You too
can be happily-married forever-after!" "Have
you found your knight in shining armor?" "God
has created one true soul mate, out there, who
is just perfect for you!" "Better to keep a
secret than to air your family's dirty laundry."

Can you imagine not telling your own Momma
that your spouse was sneaking off to attend
to his other family? That's right, Grandpa
Manlowe had two full families to take care of
(or to *be present to* in a half-assed way)! Did
you girrlees know this?

NOTE: Listen to your Tia, gally-gals; the only way you will live "happily-ever-after" is if you are as lifeless as this Barbie doll in a fairy tale. Girrrls, I'm not joking, this is serious! I wish I were kidding about the toxicity of romantic promises pitched to women and girls, but I swear to you, these bizarre oaths about marriage are just a few of the messy messages that Big Sissy and Momma passed on to me.

In the 1950s, Americans were warned to fear the "Iron Fist" of Communism. I'm not trying to scare you by warning you against some Velvet Fist called Romantic Love. But, I am saying, be mindful of those slick promises of coupled-bliss that you might hear in church or see on those diamond commercials. They are usually in service of the status quo—living a numbed out life that must be continually injected to maintain the buzz (like Heroin).

In the fall of 1990, around Alyssa and Maria's birth, I married one very funny guy, a stand up comic  (just like Robin Williams). We had a lot of fun before he took off on a bi-polar tear (just like Robin Williams) right after our first attempt at couple's therapy. I know this seems both sad and ridiculous but it happened just six months after we both said, "I do." It took me a while to re-inject the ideal that marriages could be trustworthy arrangements that were "good for all." So, about 10 years after that divorce, in July of 2001, I married again only to find out that my new spouse was a secret, night-time binge drinker who couldn't keep his *mits off der kinder* (i.e., he was rumored to be dating his very own, extremely-bright students!). Oops. Both of these men, much like me, were about as emotionally mature as Baby Huey— remember him from Nickelodeon?

For all my critical thinking, my four degrees, five languages and my 20+ years of psychotherapeutic counsel, I was no wiser than all the women who believe there's such a thing as one, true "soul mate" who could foster complete joy or, better, offer "completeness" through marriage [a mirage?]. I can't blame Momma or Big Sissy for my participation in this *folie à deux*. These women, like most women of their era [error?], were merely conduits of misery for an entire continent of family myths told to them by the well-intentioned, conservers of tradition. A little bit of background on the cult to which these women were merely fallouts is in order, yes?

SOUL MATE? DO WE EVEN HAVE A SOUL?

"The universe is made of stories, not atoms."
—*Muriel Rukeyser*

The stories about humans having a soul, (or an unchanging core self), seem to be Western preoccupations both in religions of the west and in the psychology and philosophies reiterated in the west.

Girrrls, I know you hear me speaking to you in my "professorial tone" in this section—and it won't be the last time—but, please, hear me out; you'll want to know this later, I swear.

Western culture, in general, is very much a dualistic culture of strategically-oriented, patriarchally-colonizing, rugged-individualism. What does that mean? It means that the hero-man (as subject) discovers his world (as a separate object), objectifies it, subjugates it, extends his rule by perpetuating this arrangement through divine mandate—and likes it like that.

In most East Asian cultures, especially the Buddhist and Daoist ones, the philosophies and religious practices are intergenerational, family-focused, relationally-attuned and actively-reverent toward *nature*, its seasons and the infinite cycle of life-death. Relationship with "all that is, just as it is," is what is nurtured and attended to for everyone's greatest ease of being or sense of personal, social, and environmental harmony. What is cultivated, and considered noble, is a form of increasingly-conscious, relationally-responsive and intimately-attuned toward interdependence. [You may be thinking to yourself, "FYI, Auntie, the East as opposed to the West is not some dreamy 'haven in a heartless world' for women and girls!"] But, I say, "at least these nature/creature-inclusive philosophies have a running start for identifying and supporting a future with relationally-based ethics."

In Greek philosophy and later Hellenistic-Christianity of Saint Paul, a soul or *daemon*, (inner guide, intuition or inspiring force), was understood as a cultural given. So what is cultivated and considered virtuous in this model is individual mastery, integrity and independence. This is what Westerners have been taught since Plato recollected the teachings of Socrates (399 BCE). Impenetrable wholeness, (integrity), comes from finding what your soul would have you do, for the soul is connected to wisdom (or God, if you're a Deist[7]).

---

[7] One who believes in the existence of a Supreme Being.

Socrates' reliance on what the Greeks called his "daemonic sign," an averting inner voice that he heard only when he was about to make a mistake, was this sign that prevented Socrates from entering into politics. In _The Phaedrus_ (one of the Platonic dialogues), we are told Socrates considered this to be a form of "divine madness," the sort of insanity that is a gift from the gods and gives us poetry, mysticism, love, and even philosophy itself. Alternately, the sign is often taken to be what we would call "intuition"; however, Socrates' characterization of the phenomenon as "daemonic" suggests that its origin is divine, mysterious, and independent of his own thoughts.

Even the Indian (South Asian) philosophers from the 14th Century (BCE) believed in soul—called _Atman_ in Sanskrit. The soul is the site where all karmic or meritorious acts gather to facilitate a greater or lesser birth for the next lifecycle. The soul's skillful or unskillful acts are said to move from one being to the next, not unlike computer "memory" moves from machine casing to machine casing with the miracle of "flash drives."

You might be wondering, "How is this relevant to me, Auntie?" It is important for you to know that not all cultures believe in a soul because: "No soul," ergo, "no soul mate!" So, this might help you gals understand that the pursuit of "one true love" is virtually Western in origin— therefore neither universally nor ultimately true. This might help you loosen the fantasy that such a pursuit has over you. Perhaps you'll be less distracted by the empty pursuit of permanent and eternal romantic love.... Is that possible?

Do you feel compelled to find a soul mate, dear girrrls? Do you think you have such entities "within" as souls? In the global scheme of things, it's important to think this through.

Buddhists, Confucianists and Daoists say, "Whether we have a soul or not is just more fodder for attachment and clinging to what's impermanent and unverifiable." The Dalai Lama, Tibet's spiritual and political leader says: "Cultivate the moment you're in without grasping; nurture the relations you find yourself surrounded by; adjust, skillfully, to what arises all around you and within you; and, experiment with the happiness that emerges when you expand your focus beyond self-interest." These are major messages of Eastern Wisdom. This is why your Auntie is more aligned with Eastern thought…it just makes more sense to my lived experience to cultivate these values. I think Jesus would practice and promote them as well.

"But," I hear you say, "I want to be happy, Auntie Jenn! And I've been taught that not only do I *have* a soul inside me but that *out there, somewhere,* exists my other half—my lifelong, perfect soul mate!" You're right honey-girrrls, that is exactly what you have been *taught*. And, it is a true gift of education to know that **what you learn may also be unlearned…** or at least critically examined. As Confucius told his favorite philosophy student, Yan Hui, who was stuck inside a type of "fixed" framework of thinking. He said, "Yan Hui, you'll find that letting go of one corner [of "false-consciousness"] allows the other three to drop away." But in a relentlessly, dumbed-down culture like our own, this will take great effort. You will need to conduct a vigilant search for alternative narratives of meaning, purpose, and value. Are you up for such a search? Does it seem like a smart investment to create such alternatives, my darlings?

In Momma's case, a soul mate was the guide she sought and thought she needed; it was the ideal treasure—like *Gray's Anatomy's* McDreamy—that she saw every Saturday night at the theater, *writ large…out there* on the big movie screen. For Momma, and her entire generation, this soul mate concept was just as real and just as worthy of her focus as her health or at least her "body measurements."

"Momma, do I have to get married when I grow up?"—*Auntie Jenn at age 10*

"Oh, honey, you will want to be married, one day. Once you're a big girl…I assure you."—*Momma's response*

Such is the mystification of romantic love—it is of the same ideological template as the American Dream. To be effective, such a myth must be repeated and repeated through cacophonous fiction. This manufactured "need" and its make-believe "cure" is created and sustained through advertising.
We are not born feeling inadequate to life, we are taught that we lack something essential

through stories and images in our culture and
this message (both its cause and cure) must
be reiterated constantly, verbally and visually.

IF LOVE IS THE ANSWER, WHAT'S THE QUESTION?

"To be nobody but yourself—in a world which
is doing its best, night and day, to make you
like everybody else—means to fight the
hardest battle which any human being can
fight, and never stop fighting."—e.e. cummings

"Resistance is futile, it is futile to resist it!"
—Cake[8]

Is romantic love supposed to be the answer to
all my problems? Is it supposed to be the salve
that will bring relief to all my open wounds? Will
it bring me infinite fulfillment? And, finally, am I
supposed to be happy all the time?

---

[8] An Orwellian-influenced rock band from Sacramento.

As a little girl, Momma often allowed me to stay home from school "sick" to accompany her as she watched *morning matinee*. It was super fun to be together in our secret form of indulgence. But, as I look back on the content of these movies I feel a wee bit disturbed. The dramatic plots, pitched to the "stay-at-home woman," quietly functioned to indoctrinate her to a particular kind of solution to "the problem" of being female. No matter the caliber of the film, I often noticed that most of the female lead's physical fear and financial "bad luck" seemed to be assuaged through the magic of falling in love and getting married. Romantic love was twinned with the idea that this "case was solved" by the end of the movie.

Aside from movies, where else did we females get the idea that romantic love could fill up every nook and cranny within our psychic make up? Where did we get the idea that we even have a gaping hole in need of filling to begin with[9]—one that only romantic love and marriage can satisfy? So many women I know—from age 11-77—are women-in-waiting. Even the smartest feminists I know have struggled to resist buying into this model of wholeness. They, too, experience aloneness as a chasm stretched out before them called "forever." Straight or gay, they too feel "on

---

9 Freud's answer was penis envy? Penis envy in Freudian psychoanalysis refers to the theorized reaction of a girl during her psychosexual development to the realization that she does not have a penis. Freud considered this realization a defining moment in the development of gender and sexual identity for women. According to Freud, the parallel reaction in boys to the realization that girls do not have a penis is Castration anxiety.

hold" for their sense of completeness, waiting for that perfect, romantic mate. How many of us would tolerate more than two-minutes of being placed on hold via the telephone?

Too many of us behave like the character Penelope in Homer's <u>Odyssey</u>; we wait a lifetime for Mr. Right. You remember the character Penelope in Homer's <u>Odyssey</u>, yes? She is the one in the Greek epic who weaves and unweaves a robe (to distract both herself and would-be suitors) as she awaits the return of her soldier husband, Ulysses. She convinces herself that all her worries will be over once HE returns to her from war (see illustration below).

I promise, girlies, you may think these 8th Century (BCE) myths don't apply to you, that you are different; that you're not as old-fashioned as Big Sissy or Momma. But, for the most part, most girls continue to be raised to believe that spiritual, emotional and physical *completion* comes through marriage . . . and that "good girls must wait!" "They must be chaste, modest, prim and proper and at least act like a virgin when in public!" Just look around you at your local Roman Catholic Church, the Blessed Virgin Mary (or BVM) had to stay a virgin—a permanent "good girl"—even after being married to Joseph and after giving birth to "our Lord!"[10]

 Another way to be considered a "good girl," besides imitating the BVM before and after marriage, is to commit to virginity, marriage to Christ alone, by taking "Holy Orders" as a nun—both marriages are considered by Roman Catholics to be one of the seven sacraments.

Even if you look to your various institutions of higher learning, you and your gal pals seem to

---

[10] She supposedly gave birth afterwards to another son. But who's keeping track of the laws of virginity?

want, or at least believe you want, the same thing, right? You think marriage and babies are equal to hitting the Lotto of true happiness. FYI, girrrls, Auntie's been married twice and it was more like "landing" a welfare-to-work program—no picnic—I promise you! Know this: However happy you are now—and before marriage—is as happy as you will be once you sign those legal documents. Just like a Lotto winner, you'll return to your ordinary "set-point" of happiness, I promise! Sociological studies bear this out—just read any one of John Gottman's published books on "Happy Couples."

> **The New Yorker Magazine** *(February, 27, 2006) found that "within a year, lottery winners and paraplegics have both (on average) returned most of the way to their baseline of happiness." But regret at the end of life needn't be true for you. It is up to you. The fact is that nobody else is going to change your happiness "set point." As comedian Carol Burnett says, "Only I can change my life, no one can do it for me."*

But, girrrls, did you know that marriage was in no way an institution founded on the romantic notion that two people "fell in love?" Rather it was originally a ritual for property exchange and a technique for shoring up a viable future for entire families (and sometimes whole clans). The arrangement could double your odds that "you and yours" would survive a cold winter or a marauding tribe.

When I was your age, I didn't know the literary source of the tradition of romantic love. I never examined the history of courtly love, and the lyric poetry that it inspired. Who knew it how recently this cult started, less than 900 years ago. It evolved among the aristocracy of Southern France during the Twelfth Century. Did you know that *true* romantic love was thought only possible *outside* marriage between a knight and *this* lady where it could be freely given and received—"no strings?" Although the mannerisms associated with courtly love were limited to a small social group and area, the poetry inspired by the tradition was carried throughout Western Europe, by the

troubadours in southern France, the
Minnesänger in Germany and proponents of
the *dolce stil nuovo* in Italy.[11] I'm sure you love
knowing all this, yes? So why did a tradition
of poetic songs and love letters foment such a
fantasy life for two? And, if romantic love isn't
as emotionally and physically rewarding as all
the promises claim, what keeps us enslaved to
these myths even up until this day?

PASSION'S INEVITABLE FIZZLE

Surely anyone who has ever felt a mad crush
has also felt its disappearance with greater
exposure? Heck, even time produces evidence
that men and women can't be partners forever.
Think about the natural lifespan. Isn't it mostly

---

[11] See also Beguine Spirituality.

men who drop dead without warning before women do? Women seem to be made of more enduring organs—or materials that support the organs. To wit: more than half of the male members of the Donner[12] party died of cold and starvation but three-quarters of the females survived, saved by that extra layer of fat we've been urged to get rid of.

Disenchantment always follows enchantment, right girrrlies? But even if we are the lucky ones who get to spend hours and hours together, forever, we know the highs are followed by lows—even for those of us who are happily joined at the hip (like your Uncle Tony and myself). What makes matters more

---

[12] **Donner Pass** is a site in the Sierra Nevada in northeastern California where some members of an 1844 emigrant party survived a blizzard partly by eating the dead.

complicated is to realize that those who do "couple" mostly *magnetize* their opposite type—whether male or female. When "in love," we find others on whom we can project the very traits that we're convinced we lack. Our loved one is full of what we want for ourselves—brilliant, linguistically-talented, physically agile or beautiful in ways that we admire. If we're impudently-impulsive, they're rigorously-rational, if we're a slob and on "island time," they're uptight and always prompt. You get the picture? Of course there are alternative motives for romantic coupling; many look for sameness rather than difference and end up with what they hope would be a twin or a perfect mirror of themselves. Naturally, difference in this arrangement is deemed to be a threat. But, a common given is presupposed, right?

Remember the *ME harmony* ad on "Saturday Night Live" in 2006? It was a skit that royally ripped on a super-popular, dating service called E-Harmony.com. In the skit, like in the actual dating business "E-Harmony," each character gets hooked up with their perfect mate who has EVERYTHING possible to share in common—it's as if they're identical twins, magically attracted to the same things; a match made in heaven, right? But, in the SNL version, it's called "ME Harmony.com" and the "perfect match" for each "would-be" suitor is the very same person (same actor) dressed as the "opposite" gender. Check it out: http://snltranscripts.jt.org/04/04lmeharmony.phtml

If romantic love is the answer to all our ills,
figuring out what question romantic love is
answering is as important as any insight that
could free a person from an addiction or a
disease. So give it some thought: What ill are
you hoping to cure with romantic love,
girrrleees?

Breaking up with a lover, a romantic liaison,
can be harder than quitting smoking (which is
said to be more difficult than quitting heroin).
But, unlike nicotine addiction, they do NOT
make a patch to shake off the lure of romantic
love and its heavenly, somnambulant promises.
And without some form of SSRIs, many feel
like they are in heavy crack-withdrawal. It's
almost laughable.

But, what's so funny about the end of
romantic love? Shouldn't we be devastated
that more than half of us become gravely
disappointed after the first month, year, (or,
in my case, third date!) of any romantic bond
of couple-dumb? So what's a nice girl with two
divorces and over 30 "romantic affairs" behind
her supposed to do? Might there be
something inherently-skewed with these
happy-ever-after promises? From my
experience, romantic oceans of passion fizzle
to eventual deserts—and most of us (men
too) prefer dessert to this desert! Hey,
speaking of dessert...

PART II

EVE SHOULDN'T HAVE HAD SUCH A BIG APPETITE!

"The food is awful here!" one woman says to another. "Yeah, I know it, just disgusting! And the portions are so small!"—*Annie Hall*

It's hard to believe that I could have been taught that Eve's appetite was too big. But, girrrls, this fib was told to me by my fourth-grade music teacher, Sr. Josie. She was an awkward, uncomfortable, post-Vatican II nun who insisted on wearing her too-tight nun's habit daily—something her more-liberated sisters were eager to shed. Sr. Josie chafed under the musty wool fibers of her modesty-maintaining black gown that was encircled by a bulky rope with a dangling iron cross. Soon Sister began to branch out into wearing the more flexible material of her double-knit, baby-blue or rat-gray polyester suits. Full of guff, she tried to police the myriad ways we girls would try to morph our own chaste, plaid green uniforms into something our peers might deem flirtatiously fashionable.

Sr. Josie tried to "contain" me, and girrrls like me, by punishing us and reminding us that we were "just like Eve"—disobedient, incorrigible and dangerously determined to follow our own appetitive curiosities.

After hearing this appellation, I stirred in a huge chunk of  Nestle's *Quick* chocolate powder into my 8-ounce carton of milk. I then looked up and whispered, "Eve was set up!" Sister then scowled at me and pointed for me to come up to the front of the classroom. My punishment was to recite the musical scales, *a cappella,* in front of my peers. She later appeared to regret making this request when she witnessed me gleefully hamming-it-up with broad fan kicks—just like the *Radio City Music Hall* dancers, *The Rockettes!* Much like the cartoon character Bart Simpson, I visited the principal's office quite a bit after age 10.

The Rockettes

Not too many years went by before I wondered if Sr. Josie was really onto something regarding the fierce cravings of females. After all, my Momma did seem to wrestle with her appetite like it was a well-greased pig. Her efforts to deprive herself of sweets never seemed to last long. I witnessed again and again poor Momma's willpower fade as she tried ingesting only vegetables, fruits and lean proteins. Her oath to herself would unravel, eventually. As it did so, she would furtively gobble up *Jamoca Almond Fudge Ice Cream, Frango Mint* candies, perfectly-shaped almond marzipan "vegetables," chocolate lovers frozen *Dove Bars* or *Pepperidge Farm Mint Milano* cookies before swearing them off for the umpteenth time—

and, like *Sisyphus*, get back on the treadmill the following day.

Under the cover of night, Momma struggled. Yet during the day, she appeared to be the "perfect little dieter" as if she were Audrey Hepburn herself—just living on a *One-a-Day*™ vitamin! This spiral-of-misery kept spinning Momma's whole life. There's a reason "D.I.E." is the first three letters in the word diet. Such dieting is more like self-immolation.

This obsession with becoming petite didn't just occur in Momma's time—which coincided with the beginnings of the women's movement. Ever since the 1960s, women who were most visible in the media were extremely thin, hollow-cheeked, and seemed to all look alike. It's no different today and such images are the same stereotypes that set nine-year-olds dieting and tell teenage girls their bodies will never be good enough. I know you girrrls are thinking, "Auntie, that's old fashioned. We're active girls who win awards playing sports and we don't diet or buy into the whole dieting industry scam." You may not, and good for you for resisting the 20th-21st-centuries most toxic female trend (33 billion-dollar-a-year profit industry). But, let's get honest. Being an athletic girl doesn't mean you're not weight and food obsessed.

Dr. Francis M. Berg, author of the award-winning *Children and Teens Afraid to Eat: Helping Youth in Today's Weight-Obsessed World*, points out that 2007 nutritional research shows that diet obsessions still take their tolls on young people. In a study of college women gymnasts, 75 percent had used hazardous methods to reduce their weight, and a new study at a Cincinnati university hospital finds two-thirds of pregnant teens have deficient diets. She says four-year-olds are asking, "Mommie, am I too fat?" Six-year-olds have full-blown eating disorders; as many as 80 percent of 10-year-old girls are restricting food and feeling guilty when they eat; and half of teenage girls are deficient in many essential nutrients.[13] Check this out:

The 13th annual *Slim Chance Awards*, presented Tuesday, January 22, 2007 on Rid the World of Fad Diets and Gimmicks Day, spotlight these worst diet products of the past year:

---

[13] http://www.hooah4health.com/body/fitness/slimming.htm

Slimming Slippers (Worst gadget). Advertising copy claims, "The Get Slim slippers...using reflexology science, magnets, and the laws of gravity to get slim! Increase your metabolism naturally [and] stimulate the untouched sole of the foot, thus activating the nerves responsible for digestion and eating habits

16-Plant Macerat Weight Loss Plan (Worst product). "Recent experiments have shown that the extract of the 16 plants, when combined together, can reverse the effect of calories. In other words, instead of transforming calories into fat, the calories are consumed and eliminated by natural means...some people have lost 13 pounds the first week."

Weigh Out (Most outrageous). "It doesn't matter how much weight you have to lose: 20, 40, 100, or 200+ pounds. This will change your life forever."

Hydro-Gel Slim Patch (Worst claim). "The remarkable dual fat-fighting ingredients, Fucus and Guaranine...boost your metabolism...your very own secret 'fat furnace'...helping incinerate away your repulsive excess adipose tissue.[14]

IF YOU DON'T WATCH YOUR FIGURE, NEITHER WILL HE!

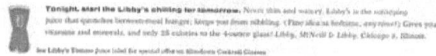

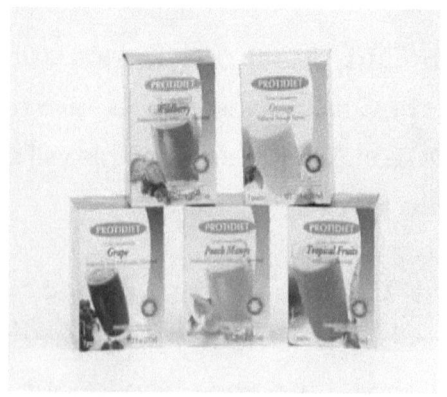

---

[14] Ibid.

Momma, like so many girls and women of her era, tried every diet trend out there: diet pills, *Ayds Candies* or diet suppressants, liquid protein drinks, the grapefruit diet, vegetable juice fasts, living on cabbage soup or ramping up on Atkin's egg whites and bacon breakfasts. She even tried sweating off the pounds—not through exercise with Jack La Lanne's TV Show—which was famous at this time. No, Momma didn't discover the value of strengthening her body until she was in her 70s with the CURVES craze.

Why didn't Momma try to "burn off" fat—as if *that* were possible—like Jane Fonda or Richard Simmons (both role-models for fitness have since confessed to their own bulimia and plastic surgery)? Because, in the

early 1970s, the ideas that magazine
advertisers pitched to women needed to be far
less-complicated and seemingly "effortless."
For instance, one could use her husband's
credit card[15] to buy a pair of "trim jeans™"!
These blow-up shorts or "sauna belts" were
something a girl could wear that promised to
"shrink her waist, hips, tummy and thighs at
least 6-9 inches in just three days.

After watching Momma's quick-fix, diet efforts fail—over 10 different methods for the first 10 years of my life—I, too, began wondering if perhaps my own appetite might need a stronger form of micro-managing. It was about that time that I learned to live on protein shakes, too. "Perhaps we could diet together," I thought to myself, "and this would keep Momma *on track* and happy."

The bad news was that I would go on to "succeed" at this dieting "craze" and would eventually mess up my endocrine system to the point of suffering from amenorrhea for most of my teens. This meant that my bones were also undernourished and many speculate that this form of malnourishment is why so many young women and girls, including me, have scoliosis emerge in their teens.

Wearing that back brace under my cheerleading uniform wasn't exactly slimming so I wore mine at night!

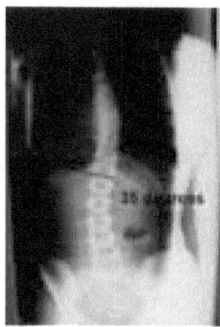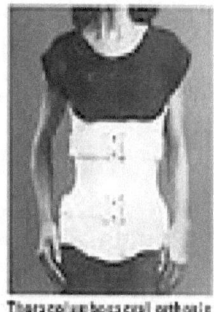

Thoracolumbosacral orthosis

Feeding oneself in any relaxed or natural way was shown to me to be something "a girl will always regret," much like having sex before marriage (and without a condom!). But, as you know, for every restriction, there is an equal and opposite rebellion. And for most women a binge is no party.

A food binge is a physiological, often nutritionally-necessary, consequence for extreme restriction and denying the need for tasty meals altogether. Unlike the men who appear to have a great time binge drinking, many women binge alone and in secret and feel not only sick the next day, but guilty for "being bad." Somehow morality gets tucked into how women use food…hmmm. I wonder why? Any guesses, girrrls?

What's tricky is "lust" for dessert for a female is only "bad," if over-indulged in. At the same time, it is understood as a good girl's acceptable substitute for sex—a form of sensual sublimation. I don't think I was alone in my habit of thinking of eating as tantamount to an "indiscretion" ... like a good Catholic girl getting caught making out in the confessional booth.

Did you know that nearly one in five Americans eats ice cream in bed? More women admit to eating ice cream in bed (22%) than the men (15%), and more women eat ice cream as a meal (29%) compared to men (19% percent). Younger women lead the pack, according to the survey. This includes eating ice cream instead of a meal; sneaking extra servings (21% compared to an average of 16%); keeping a secret stash (13% compared to an average of 7%) and eating ice cream in bed (28% compared to an average of 19%).— Survey by Harris Interactive sponsored by **Indiscretion™ Luscious Ice Cream**™.

Eat Ice Cream
Instead of a Meal
Sneak
Extra
Servings
37%
21%   28%
Eat
Ice Cream
In Bed
13%
Keep a
Secret
Stash
Ice Cream
Indiscretions
Women
18–34

Twinning ice-cream with ecstasy was something I not only saw Momma do each night but I heard her warned my 16-year-old friend, Neeta. She said, "Be careful not to have premarital sex because 'It's just like eating a Hot Fudge Sundae. You'll just want another and another so it's best not to even have one!'"

This unnatural obsession with food and weight can turn into a tragic and fruitless struggle of grand proportions — something that I elaborate upon in my first book entitled *Faith Born of Seduction*. You girls have already read that one, right? If not,

please run, do not walk to your  i-Phones™ and order it right now through New York U Press: (212) 996-2546 or http://www.nyupress.org/

NOTE: Do you think it's just a little strange that the rhyme: "Little girls are made up of sugar and spice and everything nice" – is the exact substances we are urged to resist?

For our purposes here, let's just say I have heard all too well that women, after Eve, were indeed the appetitive ones who demanded extraordinary oral-restraint if they were to be seen as civilized (read, *appropriately feminine*). Think about this, gally-gals: Why must we females fear our desires? Why must our desires be scrutinized by some amorphous, external-to-us, fault-finding gaze—something fairly familiar to a Catholic girl's "Father/God"? How do we perpetuate this culturally-inculcated, critical creature called "the internalized sexist pig gaze," as if Barbie-like appearances were what our life was to be all about?

Have you ever wondered what "gaze" you've internalized? When you look in the mirror, who do you think is looking back at you with "advice" as to what to improve? What visual cues are you obeying? Which models are you imitating when you put on make up or dress? This isn't a judgment; we all do this.

I'm just inviting you to consider your motivations so you can be transparent with yourself—an informed practitioner of beauty rituals and ideals. Is that possible?

FAVORITE MODEL:

_____

FAVORITE SPORTS HERO:

_____

FAVORITE
ACTRESS:_____

Perhaps messages like this one (below) might egg us on to live as if we were pretty seashells who prefer the shallowest of waters?

IF YOUR FRIENDS ARE FAT, YOU WILL BE TOO!

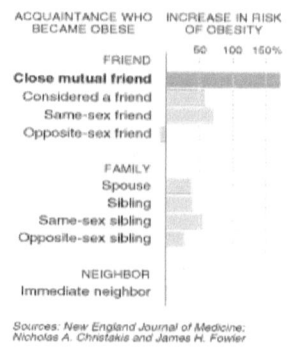

Obesity Among Friends

A study of 12,067 people over three decades found that people were at a greater risk of becoming obese when a close friend became obese.

ACQUAINTANCE WHO BECAME OBESE	INCREASE IN RISK OF OBESITY

Sources: New England Journal of Medicine; Nicholas A. Christakis and James H. Fowler

The New York Times

Perhaps we should pick our friends for their appearance too, do you think? Maybe that sexist male gaze isn't just measuring our own bodies but the bodies of those with whom we "hang." Shallow studies show: "If your friends are fat, you will be too?" Hmmmnn. Let's play a guessing game. You tell me, of the three women above, which one has tried to control her appetite by fasting? Which one "succeeded" in maintaining a weight 1/3rd below her natural body size?

a. The famous woman, the one who just happens to be slender, has successfully kept her weight below 90 pounds through a virtual-fasting lifestyle buoyed up with the help of cocaine.

b. Both women in the diaphanous tights fasted and fasted until their appetites were shot to hell and each one, (quite naturally, really), couldn't get enough to eat once she stopped fasting.

c. Both "a" and "b" are true.

If you picked "a" "b" or "c" you were correct. What kind of world demands that women take up less space? Don't you think it would be absurd to claim there is some kind of plot to keep women out of boardrooms, courtrooms, parliament, leadership and in the bedrooms, kitchen and shopping malls? Have you ever wondered why women seem to be raised to be consumers rather than producers, creators, inventors? If you look at the advertising, something you see a lot of in your piles and piles of teen magazines, it's hard not to think there's a conspiracy!

"Magazine ads are meant not only to sell products, but also to make promises and create new values and lifestyles."
—Jean Kilbourne

In the film *Killing Us Softly,* Kilbourne claims "$33 billion is made from the diet industry each year, 50 percent of American women are on diets, 75 percent of women think they are overweight, 80 percent of 10-year-old-girls are on diets, 11.3 percent of college women are on diets and the number-one wish of American girls is to lose weight and keep it off."[16]

Please learn this lesson now, gally-gals: "Diet-mentalities = death" "scales are for fish" "starving is for the brain dead." This lesson came almost too late in my life: the more control—via deprivation that I cultivated, the

---

[16] http://jeankilbourne.com/news.html

less I could focus on creating a full life. The more helpless I felt the more I returned to my most tangible asset (my self-discipline!) and the stronger was my obsession with food, weight and body size. It's true for any one of us: "What we resist, persists!"

The Buddhist sages often say, "Trust the rhythms of nature! When tired, sleep. When hungry, eat." It's that simple, girls, I promise. Most babies know how to do this.[17] But just like the story of Eve in Garden of Eden, we hear that **we're forbidden to eat** from that tree over there! You know the one, that *Tree of Knowledge between Good and Evil*.[18] The other tree in the middle of the Garden was the

---

[17] Especially those of us who live in a "first world" country.
[18] The same story is told in many Mesopotamian myths, most notably the story of the Gilgamesh Epic.

Tree of Life. What greater enticement is there than such a prohibition? Freud claimed that myths of origin were told as morality tales that veiled the fact that all humans have two roiling forces born within us as inheritors of our animal ancestors: we constantly lean towards Life and/or towards our own Destruction (some might call this Good and Evil). What human could resist?

The moral to the creation story—and the 300-plus morality tales of creation just like this one—is that "we all love to rebel!" and if it is culturally forbidden, we'll rebel in secret!

Just look what happens when Momma leaves out caramel-fudge brownies on the window sill to cool. We all know resistance is futile! I know I decided to diet-for-life when my older brother Bobby said, "Do you really think your butt can *afford* another one of those Carmel Fudge Brownies?"

CARAMEL FUDGE BROWNIES

21 1/2 oz. pkg. ANY fudge brownie mix
20 caramels
3 tbsp. Half-n-Half
1/2 c. semi-sweet chocolate chips

Prepare and bake brownie mix according to package directions.

In small saucepan over low heat (I use a double boiler), melt the caramels with 3 tablespoons Half-n-Half; stir until smooth.

Immediately, after removing brownies from oven, sprinkle with the chocolate chips. Drizzle with caramel. Cool completely before cutting.

BEFORE CUTTING...

"And with his stripes we are healed."—Isaiah 53:5

Why do you think so many Catholic teenage girls hate their bodies? Could it be that their male savior's greatest act, according to many biblical scholars, and actor/director of *The Passion of Christ*, Mel Gibson himself, was self-immolation? Check this out:

In Isaiah. 53:5 "And with His stripes," the word used for "stripes," in the Hebrew, is *chaburah*. It is in the singular, and it literally means, "a bruise," the result of a blow on the skin. In the Greek New Testament, it is *molopi* and is also in the singular, "a bruise," this reveals to us that the body, soul, and spirit of Jesus was one massive and terrible bruise. He voluntarily suffered being beaten black and blue in body, soul, and spirit, for all mankind [sic]. *Strong's Concordance*, 2250 & 3468.

Another scholar goes onto say,

"The scourging Jesus received, mangled His flesh, and produced many dozens of deep bleeding wounds in His flesh, terrible wounds that even reached and exposed Christ's bones. So we can see that Is.53v5. is speaking of something more than this scourging. The inner bruising that the kind and gentle soul of Jesus suffered during this dreadful beating, was even worse than the mangling of His flesh. He was despised and rejected by those He came to save, the inner bruising and pain of this was immense." See Luke 19: 41-44.

I see why a Catholic girl (or boy like Mel Gibson) might try to "imitate" Jesus' suffering—albeit misguidedly—through masochistic rituals. But, why do you think a "non-believer" would hurt or even cut herself? A journalist I know, Nicci Gerrard, wrote an essay in the British newspaper called *The Observer* and I've quoted her at length here:

"Adolescents have always been known to self-harm, to attack their own bodies in a cry for help and as a sign of psychological disturbance. They may cut themselves, burn themselves, bruise themselves, even, says therapist Susan Sherwin-White, break their bones. They may become anorexic or bulimic (often, eating disorders accompany other forms of self-abuse). Sometimes, they take overdoses, and end up in critical care units.

"Girls are much more likely to harm themselves than boys (boys and young men attempt suicide far less often than girls, but succeed far more often: they intend to die whereas the girls are trying to get help). In prison, women turn their rage and pain inwards, against themselves, mutilating their bodies, while the men more often harm each other.

"In many cases, carving pain on to their bodies is a way of escaping from thinking about what troubles them. Adolescents are often tormented by feelings of self-loathing, a sense of being marginal and alone.

"They're not stupid or crazy, but maybe they are trying to tell us something about their inner lives and can't find the words. So they unscrew the blade of their pencil sharpener and draw it over their skin. Blood flows. 'Look at me', they're saying. 'Look how I hurt. Look.' And we should look."

Girrrls, have you ever done anything like this? Will you talk to me, or someone who will hear you? I want to hear how you express anger and frustration and hope you'll communicate your fury in a creative way in the form of art – that's what Freud calls "creative sublimation." I want to be with you as you resist the pressures to conform to some "girl ideal" that's not even close to the truth of your audaciousness.

REBEL WITHOUT A CAUSE

"Rebellion" is an idea and a word regularly used to sell goods in advertising campaigns—

"Think different!" "Rebels wanted!" "Hey, all you non-conformists, *Obey your thirst!*" Don't follow the passive herd, "Just do it!"

> *According to Nike company lore, one of the most famous and easily recognized slogans in advertising history was coined at a 1988 meeting of Nike's ad agency. Dan Weiden, ad executive, speaking admiringly of Nike's can-do attitude, reportedly said, "You Nike guys, you just do it." The rest, as they say, is (advertising) history. With the "Just Do It" slogan spoken by deified sports figures, Nike managed the deftest of marketing tricks: to be both anti-establishment and mass market, to the tune of $9.2 billion dollars in sales in 1997.—Jolie Soloman, "When Nike Goes Cold"* **Newsweek** *(March 30, 1998).*

Believing that you are a non-conformist, in this case, reminds me of the scene in Monty Python's *Life of Brian* when the Liberation

Party crowd is encouraged to shout, "We are all individuals, we are all individuals!" and we hear an anonymous, high-pitched, little voice from the throng shout out, "I'm not!"

Girrrls, prohibition is a slippery slope—don't kid yourself that you're radically rebelling when you and all your girlfriends wear lace-and-satin, super-sexy *lingerie* as if they were clothing. There's nothing naughty about false consciousness…it's called being duped into a pretend freedom! The sexist pig says, "As long as she looks sexy to me, she can call herself whatever she wants to—just open that blouse, baby!"

It's never easy to successfully go against the grain of chauvinistic social trends of the dominant culture. But, if you're a well-educated female in a leadership position, it can be really tricky. Even this white-collar professional, Dr. Victoria Nika Zdrok, could not resist the *Victoria Secret* look. Dr. Zdrok was born in Kiev, Ukraine and became an attorney, a clinical psychologist, sex therapist and a former goodwill ambassador from the former Soviet Union. As a child, Dr. Z listened

to *Voice of America* on her father's
clandestine radio and diligently studied
English with the hope of one day coming to
North America. In 1989, at the age of 16, she
was honored as the first Soviet teenager to
visit the U.S. as a foreign-exchange student.
She arrived on an academic scholarship, as
she describes it, as "a sort of ambassador of
goodwill and perestroika and glasnost." After
acquiring her professional degrees, Dr. Z was
asked to pose as a *Playboy* Playmate,
Penthouse Pet of the Year and become an
international star of elaborate adult videos.

I wonder why she felt the urge to expose
herself to this form of fame. What do you think
she was thinking? Did she need the money?
Was her role model that 1980s *virgin-whore*
icon, Madonna? Or is this one of the major

ways a woman of her background can take up a space or land a place in history, as a nude body – not unlike the majority of famous works in the Metropolitan Museum of Art.

The corporation called *Victoria Secret* and "her" multi-billionaire designers work to sell sex alongside the anti-war movement in these not so secret "Think Pink" ads.

Like salmon fiercely struggling up stream, advertisers focus on their primary goal—to foster new consuming members of their species—or at least they die trying. It's extraordinarily-challenging to be savvy, let alone a savvy consumer. It's difficult to discern when your "resistance" or rebellion is genuinely motivated by authentic purpose or when it's just another co-opted byproduct of the particularly capitalist and nationalistic machinery of what Malcolm X called "the Man." I mean…can you believe this girrrls? Do you see the mind game or can you really "think pink"?

People may be thinking that they are the rare, the few, the proud "individuals" speaking their MIND. Pahleez! When you look back ten years

from now, do you think you'll laugh or cringe in horror? Will you, like me, shiver when you see what you claim you "stood for" as your truly unique and courageous *voice*? Lyssa and Ria—you know I'm talking to you about touting Bush as "the man!" ... not in the same way as Malcolm X would say it. Oye! Girrrls, you are not alone for going along with what you saw growing up, I promise; when I was your age and even when Hilary was your age, we were REPUBLCANS! Can you believe it, your ACLU-carrying Auntie voted **for** Reagan? And we did so—just like you girls love George Bush, Jr.—because our parents admired him! We were all so proud of him because he wasn't afraid to be OUT as a public official who was Christian (anti-gay, anti-choice, just-say-no-birth-control → can you say, "pro AIDS VIRUS?"). *Hay Caramba!* So, let's have some self-compassion here, just for a few minutes…

Remember, most of us *don't see how we are seeing* through a larger cultural lens because it's the only view we know. In fact, one student from my "Intro to Logic" class protested a philosophy lecture of mine where I made the claim that "we are all affected, indoctrinated—even converted into the religion of consumption—by images we see every day." He said, "the advertising of the dominant culture never seems to affect me; I mean, I totally ignore it, **I never even see it**!" I asked him, "Really, Jack? Would you mind telling me why you simply had to wear that *Gap* T-Shirt, those *Adidas* shoes, and that *Nike* baseball cap—the clothes you are wearing right now?"

So many of us detest the idea that our needs, values and appetites for what we call "our particular style" is created for us by mass media. I mean advertising is a 33-billion-dollar-a-year industry; who wouldn't be affected by seeing over 3000 ads per day (that's 3 years of watching TV commercials, if you were to put them back-to-back)?

But girls, the feminine ideal/ideals sold are not only unreal they are decidedly unrealizable. I promise, this is a universal trend called *consumer madness* is manufactured just for us and is perpetuated via convincing the viewer that "scarcity" is what is fundamentally true. This felt sense of *lack* is an ersatz sensation that must be buoyed up over and over through subtle and not-so-subtle machinery of advertising. If this lacuna can be filled, even temporarily, through a simple purchase, the anxiety can be quelled for a few minutes. But the cycle never ends nor is it meant to end.

This feeling that "there's something missing here" is completely constructed, especially by capitilizers/capitalists in the "1st world." And this myth is exported widely, as you know. But, a lingering sense of lack needs nuance and subtlety for our ongoing convictions of incompleteness without these costly goods and services. We simply must have it (that *Lexus*, that *Pottery Barn* household item, that latest electronic gadget, that *idol* fame, that petite body size and the $200 jeans to go with it!) or we'll die. Thus, as I've said before, this consumption-orientation—"the must have it, must have it, must have it now" apparatus—is the very same ideological "technology" that runs our *need* for romantic love. Both promise to be our total-happiness solution.

We're not stupid, girls. In fact, we have to keep consuming, consuming, consuming this fiction via movies, romantic novels or music (of thwarted-happy-ever-after love) if we're to be successfully brainwashed to believe that love, (or purchasing-lovability), is the source to all our anguish. These lessons have to be visually, emotionally and virtually *beaten* into our brains until we buy (or buy into) their glossy solutions. Even some advertisers, in *Advertising Age* (editorial, 1991), want to apologize and correct their errors:

"Clearly, it's time to wipe out sexism in beer ads; for the brewers and their agencies to wake up and join the rest of America in realizing that sexism, sexual harassment, and the cultural portrayal of women in advertising are inextricably linked."

Girrrls, isn't it time we challenge the tales that set us up to such predictable feelings of failure? Isn't it time that we interrogate what's behind the glitzy curtain of deception that gives us the sense that "there's something missing in me?" Might it serve us to investigate the very engine that makes us feel that we'll just die of emptiness if we can't find Mr. Right. We'll simply go crazy if we can't have that coveted item or that promising purchase?

 Must we "depend on the kindness of strangers" for our security? See Vivian Leigh and Marlon Brando in *Streetcar Named Desire* and you'll catch on to what happens to such women—they crack up!

Do you **see** the media and everyday reiterations of "the truth" of these force-fed fictions—something philosophers Jean Paul Sartre and Simone de Beauvoir called "False

Consciousness?" Or do you think Auntie is crazy? Or both?

I'm certain that you know there is hope for transforming this false consciousness. When we commit to taking in deeper nourishment, "*Voilà!*—we cultivate truly fulfilling lives, better relationships with each other and a deeper appreciation for our surroundings. Again, we have choices; blind consumption is not necessarily the way it *has* to be. But, where do we turn for such clarity?

Where is your authentic voice and how do you find it among the values that have been inculcated in you? Where do you begin and end in relation to your friends, coaches, teachers, parents and church? Who are your

role models?

People I admire:

in History   in Fiction

_____   _____

_____   _____

_____   _____

_____   _____

I WANNA BE JUST LIKE HER!

Did you know that Lindsey Lohan and Paris

Hilton are two of the most famous girl icons

and cocaine addicts of the 21st century – at

least on record in 2007?

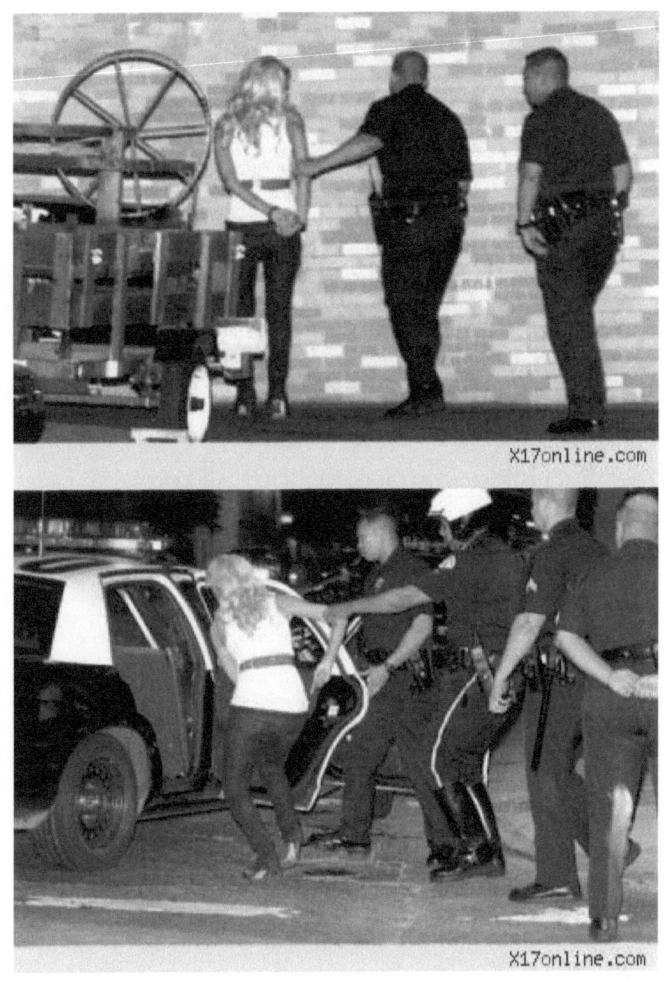

She's my heroine! Or is it my heroin?

At least they're friends...for now!

You didn't hear it from me, but did you know that according to the Buzzle, "Last Saturday Lohan reportedly showed up at Hilton's house for a post-MTV Movie Awards party. The two women reportedly had a 90-minute heart to heart and allegedly "ironed out all their differences." Now that they have discussed all their "issues," Hilton's rep says their relationship "couldn't be better."

Whatever...they'll be best friends forever until Hilton tires of Lohan or Lohan starts dating one of Hilton's many exes." Ah Young Hollywood...

PART III

GUILTY UNTIL PROVEN INNOCENT

Italian *Vogue* ad for eyeliner

My favorite Anti-Patriarchy Blogger, "Twisty," writes about Women's Dehumanization (below):

"Here's a little reminder to brighten your day: all humans are conditioned to despise women. A woman can be criticized, sentimentalized, brutalized,   infantilized,   minimized, empowerfulized, pedestalized, pornalized, and penalized, but she can never be humanized. The American legal system, as a matter of fact, effectively outlaws humanity for women. It does this in many ways, all of which define women in terms of male sexuality. One of the most insidious is its assertion that women are in a perpetual state of 'consent' unless they specify in front of 147 witnesses that they have withdrawn it (more on my radical notions about consent and women's humanity here, and even more blamer contributions here). It is by this cunning method of ascribing to women the quality of unceasing availability that the future of rape as a cornerstone of human social order is secured.

"Rape is the dominant culture's most cherished method of controlling the female underclass, of molding us into a self-replicating supply of fearful, impaired, coercible receptacles. Why else would rape trials be so notoriously torturous and humiliating for the victims? Why else would convictions be so notoriously difficult to obtain? It is *by popular demand* that, decades after American women were first deemed "liberated," the countryside remains infested with un-jailed rapists. These freely roaming terrorists are patriarchy's enforcers. They're the product of a culture of violence that luxuriates in the juridical presumption that all raped women are guilty unless proven otherwise.

"I bring this up because I recently received a long, melancholy email from "spinster niece" X who, five years after her rapist went free, is still being punished for it. After moving to a new state, X has discovered that her rapist has relocated there as well. He hasn't contacted her, so she doesn't know if he is aware of her whereabouts or not. But she is gripped with fear and loathing all the same. Her email, a sort of stream-of-consciousness blurt excerpted unedited from her personal notes, reveals that she has spent no small amount of time thinking about the rapist and the untenable situation he has put her in. In this email, X profiles her rapist exhaustively. She wonders whether his relocation is a coincidence. She describes the physical attributes of his other victims. She ponders whether he currently possesses sufficient "type-dependent psychological motivation" to seek her out. She muses about sending a friend to spy on him, about involving the FBI, about setting up a sting, about a concealed-carry permit. Reasonably and understandably, she wants to *do* something that will prevent his raping her or somebody else again, but she doesn't know what, short of buying a gun, this might entail. "I can't," she says, "let this go." So she appealed to me for "logistical/tactical/strategic advising."

"Naturally I failed her. The business of day-to-day living with the long-term repercussions of rape without shooting somebody is way out of my league. So I'm doing what I always do when I don't know what I'm doing: I'm passing the question on. Help a sister out, girls. Should you still try to remain a "good girl" when your friend's rapist goes free?"

Even the Pope John Paul gave Saint status to Maria Gioretti, a young Italian girl who submitted to death before allowing herself to be raped—thus preserving her virginity over her own life.

WHAT IS A GOOD GIRL?

It's funny how often they say to me, "Jane?"

"Have you been a good girl?"
"Have you been a good girl?"

And when they have said it, they say it again,
"Have you been a good girl?"
"Have you been a good girl?"

I go to a party, I go out to tea
I go to my aunt for a week at the sea
I come back from school or from playing a game;

Wherever I come from, it's always the same:

"Well? Have you been a good girl, Jane?"

It's always the end of the loveliest day:

"Have you been a good girl?"
"Have you been a good girl?"

I went to the Zoo, and they waited to say:

"Have you been a good girl?"
"Have you been a good girl?"

Well, what did they think that I went there to do?
And why should I want to be bad at the Zoo?
And should I be likely to say if I had?
So that's why it's funny of Mummy and Dad,
This asking and asking, in case I was bad,

"Well? Have you been a good girl, Jane?"

I've always appreciated A.A. Milne's sense of "*The Good Girl.*"

What response would you write to Jane's parents?

Here's a free-falling one that I have just spun with Uncle Tony (below). Best heard with a British accent:

DADDY'S LITTLE PRINCESS

"Piss off mum, kiss off dad, these questions you ask make me nothing but mad.

Your asking these questions persist and persist, they inspire nothing in me but the wish to resist.

These foolish queries that you lay at my door, betray that you think that I'm nothing more than a whore.

You suspicious, malicious, vacuous fools, stop making me paranoid with your vituperative rules."

I won't swallow this poop you keep dishing and dishing. Can't make me, can't make me submit to your wishing." ~ *Tony Fairbank and Auntie Jenn*

In the 1940s there was a famous song that soldiers in WWII would sing that went like this, "I want a girl, just like the girl who married dear old dad!" Yikes! Sounds like incest to me, yes? But, if you can believe it, Freud predicted that all humans suffer from what he called the *Oedipus Complex*: that nasty habit of being forever jealous of our same-sex parent and secretly wishing to "marry" our parent of the "opposite sex"—that is, if we were "normal" heterosexuals. Would this be true for you? Do you like guys or gals (or both)? Do you seem to pick ones that remind you of your dear old dad or mom (or both)? What parental traits matter most to you? Which ones (and types of men or women) do you hope to avoid? Write them down here:

Loveable Traits	Avoidable Traits
_____	_____
_____	_____
_____	_____
_____	_____

Poppa Manlowe, my dad, was a lot like Tony Soprano in that beloved HBO drama called *The Sopranos*—he was gruff, deceitful, ice-cream-stuffing, philandering, porn-profiteering, and quite sexist, really. You be the judge: once Poppa picked me up from LAX airport and told me that he had to stop by the house of a friend of his in order to pick up some money that they had made in the porn industry. I said, "Poppa Manlowe, that's gross. Those poor women are exploited and often brutalized." He scoffed, "Fat chance! All women—inside and out of the industry—are gold digging whores who use sex to secure their livelihoods." I didn't put it together, then, that Poppa was actually capitalizing on these same gold-diggin' women via his porn-investments. Hmmmm. Sexist or perfectly innocent? You decide.

He loved and identified with the characters in Mario Puzo's *Godfather*. You don't have to scratch the surface of Poppa's past too vigorously to discover that he was jumpily paranoid, rife with contradictions, but superbly "gifted" in business. For a long time, I thought Poppa might be Mafia! From my experience and from some of the slimelords and criminals he loaned money to, I think membership in *La Familia* ["the Family of Italians"] remained merely a lofty wish of his— just like the strengths he fantasized he exuded by carrying a wad of $100 dollar bills in his money clip and sleeping with a gun under his pillow. Poppa seemed to need to make people more afraid than he, himself, felt.

Poor Poppa, he didn't know we could all see
through his leather motorcycle jacket. There
was no hiding the fact that he was
psychologically fragile and quite a lonely and
frightened man. The events of September 11,
2001 pushed him over the edge. It was as if his
blossoming cancer cells quadrupled after that
date and finally took him down, organ by
organ until by March, 07, 2006, he could no
longer shake a blade of grass, let alone his
iron fist. Bless him. I hope he's at rest now that
"he is no longer with us," as they say in funeral
parlors.

One odd habit of my ole' dad, Grandpa
Manlowe, is that besides telling me that women
were "gold diggers" he also said that they were
"good for one thing and one thing only!" I
never knew what he was inferring (when he
shared this diddy with me from the ages of
about 6 to 16). But, seeing as he used to love it
when I performed "song and dance" for him

like Liza Minnelli or Barbara Streisand—my guess is women only mattered in relation to their attraction to men! So, following his lead, as a little girl, I would dress up and ham it up for him like a Las Vegas Show Girl…just like JonBenét Ramsey (above)—the cute, blond 6-year-old from Colorado who was strangled to death a few weeks before her last beauty queen contest.

Perhaps JonBenét's Poppa, just like mine, would fan the fantasies of being his "one and only" little princess. And at the time, I had no idea how this exclusive sexist attention would affect me. I didn't see inheriting my Poppa's sexist gaze as potentially crippling my sense of worth. I couldn't predict that it would mess up my body-image, my capacity to trust myself, or cripple my ability to connect with men on other levels. Such messages really took their toll; I became superbly suspicious and defensive of male attention—as if it could only be about one thing (their arousal). And so the story goes, round and round, on and on. How long? Nobody knows.

Is it tasteless to suggest of JonBenét's grisly death, rather than her career as a juvenile beauty queen, is what makes her so uncannily resemble a girl in a fairy tale? For while a pageant princess is merely tacky, a *murdered* pageant princess takes her place in the illustrious line of pretty young girls in our collective lore, to meet, or at least be threatened with, a gruesome end. Little Red Riding Hood, Goldilocks, Gretel, Alice—there is an intimate connection in our culture, it would seem, between being a sweet young miss and getting eviscerated. Just checkout any Brothers Grimm Fairy Tale.

TWISTED TALES

"Henry Darger: The Unreality of Being"
Museum of American Folk Art

According to Larissa MacFarquhar, "By curious coincidence, just after JonBenét's murder, this fairy-tale conjunction of appealing nymphets and gory murder was the subject of an unusual show at the Museum of American Folk Art in New York by the late painter and writer Henry Darger." If Darger were alive today, he would be fascinated by the story of JonBenét. Darger collected clippings on the subject of little girls, murdered and otherwise, and went on to write and illustrate a truly amazing, Scheherazadean[19] 15,145-page epic about seven cute prepubescent sisters being tormented by brutish men who like to capture little girls in order to enslave them, torture them and take their clothes off. In the course of Darger's

---

[19] Scheherazade the character who narrates the Arabian Nights. Her delightful storytelling wins the favor and mercy of her husband, the sultan of India. Every day the Sultan Shahryar (Persian: شهريار or "king") would marry a new virgin, and every day he would send yesterday's wife to be beheaded. This was done in anger, having found out that his first wife was betraying him. He had killed three thousand such women by the time he was introduced to Scheherazade who, through story telling, transformed his "moral" perspective.

story—titled *The Story of the Vivian Girls, in What is Known as the Realms of the Unreal, of the Glandeco-Angelinnean War Storm, Caused by the Child Slave Rebellion*—the sisters (the Vivian Girls) manage to escape from the men (the Glandelinians) time and time again, but countless less fortunate girl-slaves are spectacularly mutilated and slaughtered along the way.

Darger is what is known as an "outsider" artist—which is to say that he didn't receive any formal art training; was not, during his lifetime, part of the art world; and was exposed very little, if at all, to traditional art in general. As such, he is presumed to have produced his work out of some unusually pure sort of inner compulsion, rather than in response to other art. Darger spent nearly all his life living alone in a rented room in Chicago, earning his living as a janitor in a hospital during the day, going to Mass frequently, and coming home at night to work on his paintings and his writing.

Darger was born in 1892, sent to a Catholic boys' home at eight, and then placed in an institution for the feebleminded, from which he escaped at the age of 16. Shortly before his death in 1973, after Darger moved out to a nursing home, his landlord opened up his room and discovered, amid piles of presumably artistic debris (hundreds of pairs of smashed eyeglasses, balls of string, old pairs of shoes, scores of empty Pepto-Bismol bottles), one 2,600-page autobiography, an 11-year weather log, 87 watercolors, 67 pencil

drawings, and the tale of the Vivian Girls

[essay taken from www.slate.com by Larissa

MacFarquhar entitled "The Lubricious

Fantasies of Henry Darger" Posted Thursday,

Feb. 13, 1997].

THANK HEAVEN FOR LITTLE GIRLS

Girls, you might be way too young to have

seen the movie *Gigi* with Maurice Chevalier, but

do you know the song "Thank Heaven for

Little Girls?" I bring this up because this is the

song that was sung when JonBenét came

walking out onto the stage before her fawning

judges (adults, both male and female) and

other competitive little pageant members. I

wonder . . . what's so "appealing" about girls

being "helpless?

"Each time I see a little girl of 5 or 6 or 7—I

can't resist a joyous

urge to smile and

say, thank heaven

for little girls! For

little girls, get bigger,

every day —thank

heaven for little girls they grow up in the most

delightful way those little eyes so helpless and

appealing one day we will flash and send you

crashing through the ceiling – thank heaven

for little girls, thank heaven for them all no

matter where, no matter who – without them,

what would little boys do? Thank heaven,

thank heaven, thank heaven for little girls!"

PART IV

TRULY CRACKED UP!

Girrrlees, especially Molly, be warned! Who wouldn't crack up like a crazy person with all these whacky messages for girls? I know I had my fill by the time I was 18—just in time for college! Growing up is always hard to do but being filled with so many mixed messages can drive a girl insane. I'm sure you've heard something like the ones I've heard: "Be sexy but don't have sex!" "Be voluptuous (up top) but don't get fat!" "You can be smart but not too smart—it's considered manly!" "Boys are funny, but girls who say the same exact words are crude!" "Men can fool around, play the field, sow their oats, but if you're female doing the same, you're a whore!" Let's crack the code of these death-dealing myths. Or help the perpetuators of them return to their crack pipes…because we're not buying any of it!

I want to learn from you now. Please tell me how you hope to throw off all the messages that make you mad? Are there heroines out there that crack you up? That inspire you to be authentic, let your humor rip, express yourself, tell your truth, trust yourself, follow your heart's desires, listen to your gut, and be powerful and intelligent? I'd love it if you would write me a letter and let me know. I want to read your books!

HAS MY HEART GONE TO SLEEP?

Has my heart gone to sleep?
Have the beehives of my dreams
stopped working, the waterwheel
of the mind run dry,
scoops turning empty,
only shadow inside?

No, my heart is not asleep.
It is awake, wide awake.
Not asleep, not dreaming
its eyes are opened wide
watching distant signals, listening
on the rim of vast silence.—*Antonio Machado*

After reading this long letter, my prayer to all

the worlds' goddesses and gods (I just wrote

dogs! Freudian slip? I think not!) is that you

won't be too discouraged to learn that so

many of us have been raised/lulled to live half-

asleep/half-alive to our authentic appetites.

Always remember that true heart awakening

often comes in the form of a natural empathy with all beings, not just one mate as your "one and only!" It's not that romantic love is evil in and of itself. It only rots if it's glommed onto like a baby blanket that smells sweet at first but reeks without fresh air and fellowship. If pairing up in two's is just a beginning, it can open your own heart to wider forms of care for all creatures, especially if you know how to discern what's true from what is untrue and are determined to look at all of it with eyes opened wide!

SEEING CLEARLY

"People are always blaming their circumstances for what they are. The people who get on in this world are those who get up and look for the circumstances they want, and, if they can't find them, make them."
—George Bernard Shaw

Girrrlees, as you know, I've been helping girls and women just like you find ways to dial down the deceit and the stress it causes so you can see clearly what you value and how you want to live. My methods for living more closely to my creative and sensually-savoring appetites draw largely from what I have learned from Insight Meditation or Mindfulness Meditation techniques.

Insight Meditation (known in Sanskrit as *Vipashyana*) is a comprehensive approach to awakening of the heart and mind. This method of awareness training has been practiced in Asia for over 2,500 years and, because of its simplicity and power, is now being embraced by people from diverse spiritual orientations around the world. Insight meditation cultivates our natural wisdom and compassion. The practice develops concentration, which allows us to calm and steady the mind. The subject of concentration is usually the movement of the breath, or the appearing and disappearing of sound. As the mind quiets down, it is possible to experience whatever arises in the present moment in an accepting and open way. This present non-judging attention is called mindfulness, and comprises the heart of Buddhist meditation.

Mindfulness can be maintained throughout our daily activities. We can be mindful of the movement of our body, the sensations in walking, the sounds around us, or the thoughts and feelings that come into the mind. As mindfulness deepens, there is increased capacity for intimacy with the life within and around us. We are able to see through our culturally-conditioned behaviors and thoughts, and discover compassion, equanimity and freedom in our lives.

How To Meditate By Yourself[20]

Part I: How to Establish a Daily Sitting Practice

Before you sit

As with all things, start where you are. You have everything you need right now. First, decide to sit each day. Next, plan the time, place and duration for your sitting meditation.

Choose a time

Morning is often best because the mind is calmer than it is later in the day. However, the best time is the time that you can commit to on a regular basis. If one longer sit isn't possible, try two shorter ones.

---

[20] Taken from the Insight Meditation Community of Washington website:
http://www.imcw.org/getall.php?cid=12&scid=13

Choose a space

There is no perfect place. If possible, dedicate a space exclusively to your daily sitting. Choose a relatively quiet space where you can leave your cushion (or chair) so that it is always there to return to. You may want to create an altar with a candle, inspiring photos or statues. These are not necessary, but are beneficial if they help to motivate you.

Choose a duration

As long as is comfortable, plus 5 minutes. This is a general guide, not a rule. Even fifteen or twenty minutes will seem an eternity in the beginning, but that impression will change with time. If you sit each day, you will experience noticeable benefits (e.g., less reactivity, more calm) and be able to increase your sitting time.

Every time you sit:

Set your intention

It is helpful to recall at the start of each sitting meditation why you are doing it. Remember that your purpose, to become more open and free, will benefit you and those around you.

Set your posture

Alertness is one of the two essential ingredients in every meditation. Sit on a chair, cushion, or kneeling bench as straight and tall as possible. In the beginning, sitting against a wall can help you learn what a straight back feels like. Around this straight-back position, let the rest of your skeleton and muscles hang freely. Let the hands rest comfortably on your knees or lap. Let the eyes close, bringing the attention inward.

Relax deeply

Openness is the second essential ingredient in every meditation. Once you feel your spine is erect, let everything else relax, hang loose, and soften. Breathing through the nose, loosen the face, neck, hands, and stomach area. You may want to begin at the scalp and move your attention slowly downward, methodically relaxing and softening each part of the body. Please don't skip the step of relaxing/letting go! Consciously releasing body tension will help you open to whatever arises during your meditation.

Choose an object of meditation

Once you've established this alert and open posture, you are ready to decide where you'll place your attention. Useful objects for beginners include:

The breath as it enters and leaves the nostrils.

Other body changes during breathing, e.g., the **rise and fall of the chest**.

Sounds as they arise from within the body or outside of it .

Whatever object you select, stay with it for at least ten breaths. Even with this effort, your mind will insist o-n going to its usual places. Make note of this when it happens, and gently lead your attention back to the chosen object of meditation. Your intention and persistence are the key ingredients for cultivating awareness, not the number of times your mind wanders. As often as you need to, check yourself—"Alert and erect? Relaxed and

open?"—and begin again.
The classical objects of meditation:

The four objects of meditation that the
Buddha outlined in the *Satipatthana Sutta* are
called the four foundations of mindfulness or
the four frameworks for cultivating
mindfulness. They are:

Mindfulness of the body (starting with
breath).
Mindfulness of feeling (there are 3 - pleasant,
unpleasant, and neutral).
Mindfulness of mental objects (thoughts and
emotions).
Mindfulness of all dharmas (all phenomena),
starting with the 5 hindrances and the 7
factors of enlightenment and proceeding to all
the sense and thought experiences that make
up human life.

A different object of meditation:

Metta practice, also called loving-kindness
meditation, cultivates both compassion and
concentration. The practice uses specific
phrases to send loving and kind wishes to (a)

yourself, (b) your parents, (c) your teachers or mentors, (d) your family, (e) your friends, (f) neutral persons, (g) difficult persons (or enemies), and (h) to all beings everywhere, without exception. The phrases might be:

May I be filled with lovingkindness. May I be safe from harm. May I be well. May I be peaceful and at ease. May I be happy. May my parents be filled with loving-kindness. May they be safe from harm...(etc.)

To learn more about metta meditation, read *Lovingkindness* by Sharon Salzburg.

Concentration and mindfulness:

It will be important as you practice to recognize and balance the qualities of concentration and mindfulness. Concentration is the ability to gather your attention into one place. Mindfulness is pure moment-by-moment noticing. Without some concentration, mindfulness is difficult to sustain. Without mindfulness, concentration bears no fruit. In meditation practice, both are developed gradually.

Part II: Common Issues for Meditators

Monkey Mind: At first, you may be surprised at how active and uncontrolled your mind is. Don't worry ~ you are discovering the truth about your current state of mind. Accept and "sit with" whatever comes up. Don't try to change it by force, use patience. Sit up, relax, and gently bring your attention back again and again to the object of your meditation.

It is common to mistake thinking for meditating. It takes practice to distinguish pleasant, dreamy thoughts from having your attention connected to the changing experience of this moment. Staying focused on the body/breath is a good way to stay grounded in the present.

The classical five hindrances to practice are:

Grasping: wanting more (or something different) from what's present right now.

Aversion: fear, anger, any form of pushing away.

Restlessness: jumpy energy, agitation.
Sloth and torpor: sleepy, sinking states of

mind and body.

Doubt: a mind-trap that says, "it's no use, this will never work, maybe there's an easier way."

Meditators experience all of these states. During sitting practice, if you notice one of the hindrances arising, it is useful to name it silently to yourself, e.g., "grasping, grasping" or "sleepy, sleepy". If it is strong, try not to pull away from the difficult energy, but bring all of your attention to it. Let yourself experience it fully through the sensations in your body, neither getting lost in it nor pushing it away. Watch what happens without expectations, and when it dissipates, return to the primary focus of your meditation.

Part III: Sustaining a Practice

Here are just a few helpful hints for sustaining your sitting practice: Sit every day, even if it's for a short period.

A few times during each day, establish contact with your body and breath. Practice regularly with a group or a friend.

Kittens, you now know, first hand, that "truth is stranger than fiction." Not one true story that I have shared with you in this letter needs to be true for you. Just remember what my friends in A.A. say, "Take what you like and leave the rest." Remember, too, that this book was written in the spirit of Gertrude Stein who said, "I do not write in order to be right!" I hope you'll let me know what messages have supported or hindered your own experiences of "growing up female." I bet you gals and your gal-pals could weave a tale or two that would have us all cracking up. So please know this: I await your letters with eager delight!

Forever yours,

Auntie Jenn
1 December 2007
Bainbridge Island, WA
http://MyLifeDesignUnlimited.com

www.ingramcontent.com/pod-product-compliance
Lightning Source LLC
Chambersburg PA
CBHW031323290526
45784CB00014B/941